Classic of Accusation

Handbook of Ancient Chinese Conspiracies
and Frames, "Luo Zhi Jing" 罗织经

by

LAI JUNCHEN 来俊臣 (651 - 697)

Translated and Edited by
LINGKAI KONG 孔令恺

IIOPS

Istanbul Institute of
Political Strategy

CLASSIC OF ACCUSATION: HANDBOOK OF ANCIENT CHINESE CONSPIRACIES AND FRAMES, "LUO ZHI JING"

罗织经

CONTENT

This page intentionally left blank.

THE TRANSLATOR

Lingkai Kong. A PhD candidate in Political Science, Izmir University of Economics, Turkey. He received his bachelor degree in Economics from Beijing Foreign Studies University, China, and master degree in Economics from the University of Zurich, Switzerland.

He is the author of the book *The Philosophical Reviews of International Politics*. He translated and edited the book "Luo Zhi Jing" - *Classic of Accusation* into English version for the first time. He also retranslated and edited the English version of the book *The Art of War* to make it more accurate and readable, and substantially revised the Lionel Giles's version that was in circulation. He is the manager of the *Journal of Politics and Strategy* and co-founder of the Acik Demokrasi ve Bilim Vakfi (Open Democracy and Science Foundation). He is a reviewer and editorial board member for several journals.

He used to publish articles in *Mathematical and Statistical Economics*, *Journal of Mathematical Finance*, and *Journal of Quantitative Finance and Economics*, etc. Now he has moved into the field of political science. His main areas of research include federalism, political philosophy, and democratic theory.

He has two cats named Afu and Huzi.

ACKNOWLEDGEMENT

This book meets readers for the first time in English. Due to the difficulty of ancient Chinese, translators must first translate it into contemporary Chinese and then into English. Fluency and readability must be considered during the translation process, as well as making the text as elegant as possible. Changling Kong and Wenxian Lee assisted the author during the translation process.

Thanks for the support from Acik Demokrasi ve Bilim Vakfi (Open Democracy and Science Foundation). Thanks for the Istanbul Institute of Political Strategies to edit and publish this book.

This publication is available in paperback format with ISBN 978-1-7392712-4-4, and also available in ebook format on several platforms. If some reader want a hardback edition, please contact the author   at

lingkai.kong@std.izmirekonomi.edu.tr or
konglingkai098@gmail.com.

Readers are welcome to point out any
errors.

Lingkai Kong
2023 in Izmir, Türkiye

PREFACE

Due to the lack of legitimacy of her administration, Wu Zetian, a legendary female empress of the Tang Dynasty of China, kept a strict watch over her subjects after becoming ruler. As a result, she urged her ministers to watch and snitch on one another, and she established special organizations to apprehend dissidents. This period was known as "Kuli politics," and the "Kuli" was a brutal and vicious justice enforcer - like secret police. They frequently served as imperial power protectors by scheming to fabricate and falsify evidence. By the conclusion of Wu Zetian's reign, the "Kuli politics" had become so out of hand that the emperor herself had to execute these renowned Kuli.

Lai Junchen 来俊臣 (651 - 697)

In 690-692 A.D., the author of this work, Lai Junchen, rose to prominence. And quickly became the leader of the organization of covert police agents. Lai Junchen epitomizes the two qualities of the secret police: the ability to accurately record and fabricate crimes, and the use of great cruelty in persecuting people.

Zhou Xing is another police group leader.

After being manipulated by Emperor Wu Zetian, he was ultimately put to death by his comrade Lai Junchen. Lai Junchen invited Zhou Xing to dinner and asked him, "Why so many inmates refuse to confess? Is there any way to make them confess?" Zhou Xing stated, "This is simple; get a large stove, ignite a fire below it, and place the prisoners inside. They are unable to endure the anguish and will confess." Lai Junchen then promptly requested a large stove and said to Zhou Xing, "I now accuse you of rebellion; please enter the stove." The ruthless prosecutor Zhou Xing was ultimately killed by his colleagues. When Zhou Xing was dying, he read *Classic of Accusation* - the " *罗织经 Luo Zhi Jing*" authored by Lai Junchen, and thought that his brutality was indeed lesser to that of Junchen, thus he accepted his death peacefully. Later, the book *Classic of Accusation* "Luo Zhi Jing" was passed on to Monarch Wu Zetian. After the monarch saw it, she sighed: "Such calculations and manipulations! Even I may not be able to compete with him." Consequently, the monarch considered executing Lai Junchen.

In the of thousands of years of Chinese history, *Classic of Accusation* is an unique text with an exceptional significance. First, it is the first masterpiece on the topic of establishing unjust prisons since the dawn of humanity. Second, it is the first admittance of wickedness by a cruel official. Thirdly, it is the first full book of tricks in the history to collect wicked wisdom. Fourth, it explains for the first time why deceitful officials live better than loyal ones: underhanded schemes and lack of shame.

This translation of *Classic of Accusation* introduces this work to English-speaking audiences for the first time. In China, *Classic of Accusation* has a respectable reputation, although it is not well-known elsewhere. Information about the *Classic of Accusation* in English is equally fractured and disorganized. Written in ancient Chinese around the end of the seventh century, it will be challenging even for overseas readers who understand Chinese. Therefore, the translator chose to edit this book into fluent English so that it might be read by everyone. The purpose of publishing this book is not to persuade people to use power and conspiracies to frame others, but to understand the complex and dark side of ancient officialdom and the fact that everyone in the imperial power system is a victim of political struggles, including the emperor's favorite minister like Lai Junchen. Victims of the power struggle between the imperial power and the nobles were the common people. Now that the republic system transfers political power to the people, through the representative system. We are far away from the ancient court struggles, therefore it is possible that conspiracies and shadowy politics have become alleviated, right? Maybe.

Following the English translation is the original Chinese text, which is written in ancient Chinese. Given that ancient Chinese is marked by brevity and richness of substance, the length appears to be short. The translator has numbered each paragraph so that the reader may compare the English and Chinese versions.

Lingkai Kong
2023 in Izmir, Türkiye

1. Insight into Others

This page intentionally left blank.

1. Insight into Others

阅人卷

1. **Insight into Others**
阅人卷

(1) How can people be trusted when so many of their emotions are delicate and so many customs are hypocritical? Confucius[1] stated, "Zuo Qiuming[2] considers pretending sweet words, pleasant expressions, and reverence to be despicable, and I concur." It is

---

[1] Confucius. He was the Spring and Autumn Period Chinese philosopher who founded the Confucian school of thinking. Successive monarchs or adherents of Confucianism have venerated Confucius as a sage. China and East Asia have been tremendously influenced by Confucianism.

[2] Zuo Qiuming. Per the mythology, at the end of the Spring and Autumn Period in China, he was a blind historian from the State of Lu and the creator of *The Commentary of Zuo* and *Discourses of the States*. During the Warring States period, *The Commentary of Zuo* became a classic of the Confucian school.

disgraceful for someone to be deceitful when they appear pleasant to others but are actually resentful on the inside.

(2) Human nature is selfish, and human desires are diverse. When things succeed, people take credit, but when they fail, they place the blame on others, not even the saints can surpass this. This is probably the inexorable result of human nature.

(3) Excessive desire develops greed, extreme selfishness produces deviance, from which conditions evil emerges. People fear punishment, and officials fear danger; hence, they have to restrict their behavior. Once change is possible, nobody can foresee their conduct.

(4) People are frequently harmed because they do not observe closely, and they frequently experience disaster as a result of unnecessary mercy. Duke Huan of

1. Insight into Others

Qi[3] pampered his subjects excessively and suffered a terrible death as a result. King Fuchai of Wu[4] did not acquire the kingdom of Yue, but ultimately caused the decline of his own empire. There is no tighter tie than that between father and son, yet a wayward son like Yang Guang[5] always exists; there is no bigger honor than that

---

[3] Duke Huan of Qi (? - 643 BC). The ruler of the Qi state during the Spring and Autumn era. He appointed sage professionals, cultivated productive forces, eradicated political corruption, and enhanced military capabilities. Under his direction, the state of Qi became the first hegemon within ancient Chinese territory. In the latter years of his reign, his nomination of disloyal ministers caused such havoc in the dynasty that he was imprisoned and starved to death in his palace by the traitors. After his death, his sons descended into internecine conflict, and the empire declined.

[4] Fuchai (? - 473 BC). King of the Wu State during the Spring and Autumn Period. Under his leadership, the State of Wu defeated the State of Yue, an ancient adversary; nevertheless, due to his generosity, he did not entirely destroy the State of Yue but instead imprisoned its ruler. Later, the monarch of the Yue State avenged Fu Chai by conquering the Wu State.

[5] Yang Guang (569 - 618). The second emperor of China's Sui Dynasty. According to legend, he killed his father, the elderly monarch Yang Jian, and usurped power when his father was gravely sick. The old king Yang Jian is regarded as one of history's greatest monarchs.

monarch give to his subject, yet treacherous ministers like Wang Mang[6] keep emerging. Thus, it is stated that the human mind contains so much deceit that one cannot judge someone just by his appearance. The world lacks warmth and love, and those who perform good deeds are not recognized. It is preferable to believe in oneself rather than others, and to take precautions rather than taking chances. How could a person become wise without mastering these skills?

【The original text in ancient Chinese】
【中文原文】

---

[6] Wang Mang (45 BC - 23). A prominent Chinese statesman during the Western Han Dynasty. Initially, he was acclaimed for being a respectful and morally upright minister. But upon attaining power, he eventually exposed his ambition, abolishing the Western Han Dynasty and establishing the Xin Dynasty as his own state. He is a disputed historical figure in China. During his ascent to the throne, he crushed dissenters, selected cronies, and implemented several reforms that were so ahead of their time that they were ridiculed by the people. His empire eventually succumbed to insurrection, and he was murdered by the rebels.

1. Insight into Others

(1) 人之情多矫，世之俗多伪，岂可信乎？子曰："巧言、令色、足恭，左丘明耻之，丘亦耻之。"耻其匿怨而友人也。

(2) 人者多欲，其性尚私。成事享其功，败事委其过，且圣人弗能逾者，概人之本然也。

(3) 多欲则贪，尚私则枉，其罪遂生。民之畏惩，吏之惧祸，或以敛行；但有机变，孰难料也。

(4) 为害常因不察，致祸归于不忍。桓公溺臣，身死实哀；夫差存越，终丧其吴。亲无过父子，然广逆恒有；恩莫逾君臣，则莽奸弗绝。是以人心多诈，不可视其表；世事寡情，善者终无功。信人莫若信己，防人毋存幸念。此道不修，夫庸为智者乎？

— 8 —

This page intentionally left blank.

2. Serving Superiors

事上卷

2. Serving Superiors
事上卷

(5)   When a superior's suspicion is heavy, fear arises in the subordinate. When superiors and subordinates do not share the same mind, misery ensues.

(6)   If a superior is prideful, obey him to bring him peace of mind. If a superior is anxious, show loyalty to prevent him from suffering. Do not shy away from flattery in obedience, do not shy away from being unreasonable in loyalty, and do not stop even if others defame you. Everything you receive will originate from your superiors. How can you go against them if your life and death are in their hands? Therefore, wise people are adept at surreptitiously

predicting the thoughts of their superiors, whilst idiots exclusively adhere to their own beliefs. This factor accounts for the disparity between their good and bad fate.

(7)   Superiors do not like those subordinates who are too powerful. Subordinates should abstain from the idea of pursuing excessive power. Too much power for a subject will lead to death, and absurd ideas will lead to destruction. Even mighty minister as the Duke of Zhou, Ji Dan[7], was cautious because of fear of being suspected, let alone other people.

(8)   No superior lacks wisdom, and no inferior has the most morality. Give the credit to your superior and keep the blame to yourself. Do not lose your alertness and do not demonstrate your intelligence and

---

[7] Ji Dan (? - about 1000 BC). He was active around the year 1000 BCE. He was one of the Western Zhou dynasty's founders. He supported the young emperor in constructing the empire's institutions and was the empire's true ruler. In order to prevent suspicion, he displayed extreme humility due to his immense authority.

courage. Even for those close to you, you are cruel, and even if it is a evil thing against your principle, you obey orders. If you truly carry out this action, not only will your superior appreciate you more, but your favor[8] will not diminish.

【The original text in ancient Chinese】
【中文原文】

(5) 为上者疑，为下者惧。上下背德，祸必兴焉。

(6) 上者骄，安其心以顺。上者懦，去其患以忠。顺不避媚，忠不忌曲，虽为人诟亦不可少为也。上所予，自可取，生死于人，安能逆乎？是以智者善窥上意，愚者固持己见，福祸相异，咸于此耳。

(7) 人主莫喜强臣，臣下戒怀妄念。臣强则死，念妄则亡。周公尚畏焉，况他人乎？

---

[8] Favor is a term used throughout the text to describe gathering glory and obtaining the trust and affection of the ruler.

(8) 上无不智，臣无至贤。功归上，罪归己。戒惕弗弃，智勇弗显。虽至亲亦忍绝，纵为恶亦不让。诚如是也，非徒上宠，而又宠无衰矣。

3. Ruling Subordinates

治下卷

3. Ruling Subordinates
治下卷

(9) There are few voluntarily subservient individuals. If the superior handles the subordinate without strategy, the subordinate will either oppose the superior or seize the superior's power.

(10) If the superior lacks majesty, the subordinates will produce crisis. Majesty is built by etiquette and punishment; it will be lost if left neglected. Do not allow anyone to participate in plot, and afterwards eliminate those who do. Favor should not be bestowed on a single individual; allowing a single individual to dominate power would always lead to danger. Your intellect must be concealed, and connection with others should not

be very intimate. I hope that the superior's magnificence inspires respect in the subordinates.

(11)   Superiors rely on their subordinates to acquire notoriety, while subordinates rely on their superiors to realize their ambitions. If a subordinate has desires, he will naturally want advancement. The ascent should be gradual since he will be slack if he is promoted too rapidly. If the superior wants assistance, he must have a pleasant personality, treat his subordinates with respect, and not shirk responsibilities; otherwise, no one will follow him.

(12)   People have desires, and seducing them with things they like will surely succeed. People have things to fear, and exploiting those fears to persecute them, nobody will refuse your conditions. Talented people can be utilized: if they do not pose a significant threat, they can be tolerated; if they cannot be controlled, even those with exceptional skill should be

eliminated. Don't be frugal with awards: utilize these to weaken their resolve. Punishment should be administered promptly so that subordinates can be reprimanded. Favor and deterrent are executed together, and morality and ability are compared jointly. If you do these things, you will not fail unless God wants to punish you.

【The original text in ancient Chinese】
【中文原文】

(9)　　甘居人下者鲜。御之失谋，非犯，则篡耳。

(10)　　上无威，下生乱。威成于礼，恃以刑，失之纵。私勿与人，谋必辟。幸非一人，专固害。机心信隐，交接靡密，庶下者知威而畏也。

(11)　　下附上以成志，上恃下以成名。下有所求，其心必进，迁之宜缓，速则满矣。上有所欲，其神若亲，礼下勿辞，拒者无助矣。

(12)　　人有所好，以好诱之无不取，人有所惧，以惧迫之无不纳。才可用者，非大害而隐忍。其不可制，果大材而亦诛。赏勿吝，以坠其志。罚适时，以警其心。恩威同施，才德相较，苟无功，得无天耶？

4. Manipulation of Power

This page intentionally left blank.

4. Manipulation of Power

控权卷

4. Manipulation of Power
控权卷

(13) Power is indispensable for people. Obtaining power is tough, and retaining it is even more so. People who are deficient in intelligence cannot attain power, and people who have inappropriate strategies for power will eventually bring disaster to themselves. This is a matter of life and death.

(14) Using the heaven's will as inspiration, your acts are consistent with the right path. If you defy the heaven, you must carry your own crimes - this is the sin we impose on our adversaries. It is prudent for those in authority to keep the masses in the blind, otherwise, it will be impossible to compel them to comply; the favor

must be spread out, otherwise it will be difficult for people to follow you.

(15) In a time of chaos and unrest, competent people should be utilized; once the world is peaceful, they must be eliminated to avoid future problems. During times of high prosperity, only those who are devoted to their superiors are maintained, since those who are merely average are the easiest to control. The name of position may be altered, but the real power must be held; if the name is diametrically opposed to the real power, the power will finally be lost. A person who values power over his own life can do anything. There are a variety of tactics to battle for power, as it is not voluntarily surrendered to others. Timing is crucial, if you act at the wrong time, you will put yourself in danger. Superiors should use money and luxury to constrain subordinates to reduce the actual damage they may create; reward them with fake identities

in order to gain their trust. If you follow such a strategy, you will always be in power.

【The original text in ancient Chinese】
【中文原文】

(13)　权者，人莫离也。取之非易，守之尤艰；智不足弗得，谋有失竟患，死生事也。

(14)　假天用事，名之顺也。自绝于天，敌之罪也。民有其愚，权有其智。德之不昭，人所难附焉。

(15)　乱世用能，平则去患。盛事惟忠，庸则自从。名可易，实必争；名实悖之，权之丧矣。嗜权逾命者，莫敢不为；权之弗让也，其求乃极。机为要，无机自毁；事可绝，人伦亦灭。利禄为羁，去其实害；赏以虚名，收其本心。若此为之，权无不得，亦无失也。

5. Subduing the Enemy

制敌卷

5. Subduing the Enemy
制敌卷

(16)   Everyone has enemies. A enemy is a person whose goals are in opposition to yours and whose life and death are incompatible with you. If you cannot identify your enemy, you cannot identify your allies. If you cannot defeat the enemy, you cannot advance in your field. This is the biggest evil which must be eliminated.

(17)   When a gentleman beenemys a villain, he becomes a villain himself. When a villain befriends a gentleman, he transforms into a gentleman. Fame is inconsequential, and wise people don't care about the slander and praise of others; interests are paramount, and only fools desire a

good reputation.

(18)　The common adversary of individuals do not have to be considered my enemy; but, the superior's enemy, who is even my friend, must be considered my enemy. It cannot be stated that I should be closest to my relatives, since even though the victim is my relative, the penalty must continue to be carried out. Inadvertently mislead your enemies so you can bide your time. To anticipate a favorable chance, subdue the enemy when he is immobile. It is a heinous sin to frame the enemy for revolt. It is a loathed sin to frame the enemy for obscenely. The big danger is not knowing who your enemy is; the greatest danger is becoming friends with a true enemy without realizing it. If you view every one in the world as a thief, your family as stranger, and your friend as foe, yet you are able to escape danger without any loss, right?

【The original text in ancient Chinese】

【中文原文】

(16)　人皆有敌也。敌者，利害相冲，死生弗容；未察之无以辨友，非制之无以成业。此大害也，必绝之。

(17)　君子敌小人，亦小人也。小人友君子，亦君子也。名为虚，智者不计毁誉；利为上，愚者惟求良善。

(18)　众之敌，未可谓吾敌；上之敌，虽吾友亦敌也。亲之故，不可道吾亲；刑之故，向吾亲亦弃也。惑敌于不觉，待时也。制敌于未动，先机也。构敌于为乱，不赦也。害敌于淫邪，不耻也。敌之大，无过不知；祸之烈，友敌为甚。使视人若寇，待亲如疏，接友逾仇，纵人之恶余，而避其害，何损焉？

6. Maintain Favor

固荣卷第六

6. Maintain Favor
固荣卷第六

(19)   Prosperity and favor always have a beginning, but few can last to the end; danger and inauspiciousness are not permanent, and only the wise can prevent them. Prosperity and favor are not a normal part of life; rather, they are the result of careful preparation; both danger and inauspiciousness are selected by people, and only through prudence can crises be averted.

(20)   Do not defy the monarch's command, as this is the source of favor; sensible people would rather sacrifice themselves to maintain favor. Future generations are not lacking in talent, but only favor will endure. Wise people are prepared to suffer adversities for

the sake of future generations. The only way to get an official position is to please the monarch with one's wit since a monarch always socialize with favored subjects, even for no apparent reason. Everyone has relatives, therefore when penalizing someone, you must study his family thoroughly. Distinguish between wise and foolish people, and do not enroll someone whose abilities exceed your own.

(21) Obtaining favor is envied, but it can also cause resentment from everyone. Naturally, resentment will reduce if you show your satisfaction to your superiors and extend favors to your subordinates. Large enemies must be eliminated, and reprehensible villains must not be underestimated, so that crises cannot be concealed. Joy and rage ought to be unseen. If you think carefully and maintain a far perspective, it will be tough to plot against you.

【The original text in ancient Chinese】
【中文原文】

(19)　荣宠有初，鲜有终者；吉凶无常，智者少祸。荣宠非命，谋之而后善；吉凶择人，慎之方消愆。

(20)　君命无违，荣之本也，智者舍身亦存续。后不乏人，荣之方久，贤者自苦亦惠嗣。官无定主，百变以悦其君。君有幸臣，无由亦须结纳。人孰无亲，罪人慎察其宗。人有贤愚，任人勿求过己。

(21)　荣所众羡，亦引众怨。示上以足，示下以惠，怨自削减。大仇必去，小人勿轻，祸不可伏。喜怒无踪，慎思及远，人所难图焉。

7. Self-preservation

保身卷

7. Self-preservation
保身卷

(22) The truth of the world is that people are injured by others, not themselves; others will not forgive people, but people can forgive themselves.

(23) A gentleman values his reputation, whereas a villain values his interest. If you value reputation, you will limit your conduct, but if you prioritize your interests, you will not be hindered. If renown and virtue are not exhibited, defamation cannot destroy you; if righteousness and compassion are not exhibited, deceitful and wicked people will not view you as a danger. Publicly, laud others and place him in a humiliating situation; privately, target his

7. Self-preservation

weakest spot without revealing yourself.

(24)   The average folks should not engage in conflict with the government, and the wealthy and nobility should not hold grudges against others easily. As a weak person, one must preserve life and cannot display anger; as a strong one, one must restrain his might and cannot pursue perfection. You should criticize yourself so severely that the sympathy of the crowd for you will save you from a more severe punishment. Do not penalize people excessively, as minor favors can occasionally result in large rewards.

(25)   There is no defined sentence for evil, and those who do not view evil as evil will receive favor; similarly, there is no fixed sentence for good, and those who do not view good as good will achieve peace. If you pity yourself, others will pity you; if you despise yourself, others will also despise you. If there is no stagnation and

hindrance in thinking, the scourge cannot invade you.

【The original text in ancient Chinese】
【中文原文】

(22) 世之道，人不自害而人害也；人之道，人不恕己而自恕也。

(23) 君子惜名，小人爱身。好名羁行，重利无亏。名德不昭，毁谤无损其身；义仁莫名，奸邪不以为患。阳以赞人，置其难堪而不觉；阴以行私，攻其讳处而自存。

(24) 庶人莫与官争，贵人不结人怨。弱则保命，不可作强；强则敛翼，休求尽善。罪己宜苛，人怜不致大害。责人勿厉，小惠或有大得。

(25) 恶无定议，莫以恶为恶者显；善无定评，勿以善为善者安。自怜人怜，自弃人弃。心无滞碍，害不侵矣。

8. On Loyalty and Deceitfulness

察奸卷

8. On Loyalty and Deceitfulness
察奸卷

(26)　A minister who is deceitful cannot confess himself, and a minister who is faithful cannot defend himself. Deceitful minister destroy the empire, while faithful ministers destroy themselves.

(27)　Without resourcefulness, one cannot become deceitful, because their resourcefulness is sinisterity. Faithful people will not become traitors since they have not lost their conscience.

(28)　If the resourcefulness is not greater than that of a deceitful minister, it will be impossible to conquer him; if the conscience is not profound and broad, it will be difficult to resist the deceitful.

8. On Loyalty and Deceitfulness

Loyal and deceitful ministers can be changed: People who are trusted by the monarch are regarded as loyal even though they are deceitful; those who are abandoned by the monarch are regarded as deceitful even though they are loyal.

(29) People change as the times change, so do the deceitful ministers. It is challenging to establish firm criteria for loyalty and wickedness, therefore, only the monarch can be trusted. The feelings of like and dislike will allow ministers to act deceitfully. Being the enemy of all, even those who are not traitors are considered traitors; being the friend of all, even those who are traitors are considered loyal.

(30) Two people with the same moral righteousness can gain common benefits, while moral righteousness is different only to get danger. Being a traitorous minister is advantageous, thus people may become traitors; being a loyal minister results in tragedy,

so people stop being loyal. It is true that there are many deceitful ministers and few loyal ones; it is hypocritical to claim that you are loyal and despise deceitful politicians.

(31)   The ultimate priority is to please the monarch and pursue substantive interests irrespective of one's reputation for superficial pursuits. That is how the traitorous minister's personality is revealed.

【The original text in ancient Chinese】 【中文原文】

(26)   奸不自招，忠不自辩。奸者祸国，忠者祸身。

(27)   无智无以成奸，其智阴也。有善无以为奸，其知存也。

(28)   智不逾奸，伐之莫胜；知不至大，奸者难拒。忠奸堪易也。上所用者，奸亦为忠；上所弃者，忠亦为奸。

8. On Loyalty and Deceitfulness

(29) 势变而人非，时迁而奸异，其名难
恃，惟上堪恃耳。好恶生奸也。人
之敌，非奸亦奸；人之友，其奸亦
忠。

(30) 道同方获其利，道异惟受其害。奸
有益，人皆可为奸；忠致祸，人难
为忠。奸众而忠寡，世之实也；言
忠而恶奸，世之表也。

(31) 惟上惟己，去表求实，奸者自见矣。

9. Stratagem and Trick

This page intentionally left blank.

9. Stratagem and Trick
谋划卷

9. Stratagem and Trick
谋划卷

(32)   If the monarch does not use tricks to control his subjects, some subordinates will not be able to be governed; if subordinates do not use tricks against the monarch, it will be difficult for them to advance in their official positions; and if officials do not use tricks to deal with their colleagues, they will not eliminate their enemies. In the officialdom, there are no lasting friends, and misfortunes are constantly ephemeral. This is an unavoidable circumstance, thus smart people cannot take it lightly. If you want to forecast the enemy in minute detail, you must prepare as early as possible; if you want to totally destroy your enemies, you must be merciless in planning. It is

a grave offense to cheat the monarch, so if you force others to commit this crime, he will not be spared. It is not allowed to have transgressions, so indulge someone to be trapped and accuse him.

(33) The monarch utilizes his power to plan his courtiers, and when his power is weak, he must rely on stratagem. The subordinates utilize stratagem to plan their monarch, and when the stratagem is exhausted they turn to power. The courtiers utilizes trick to deceive their peers and employ force when trick is deceived. The most essential requirement is to maintain secrecy, if you can't, you injure yourself. Transform your enemy's virtues into crimes and shaken his foundations; fabricate a ridiculous comment to falsely accuse him of saying it would enhance people's disgust toward him. Don't you have no opponents if you continue to plan so?

【The original text in ancient Chinese】
【中文原文】

(32) 　上不谋臣，下或不治；下不谋上，
其身难晋；臣不谋僚，敌者勿去。
官无恒友，祸存斯虚，势之所然，
智者弗怠焉。料敌以远，须谋于今；
去贼以尽，其谋无忌。欺君为大，
加诸罪无可免；枉法不容，纵其为
祸方惩。

(33) 　上谋臣以势，势不济者以术。下谋
上以术，术有穷者以力。臣谋以智，
智无及者以害。事贵密焉，不密祸
己；行贵速焉，缓则人先。其功反
罪，弥消其根；其言设缪，益增人
厌。行之不辍，不亦无敌乎？

10. Conspiracy to Frame

问罪卷

10. Conspiracy to Frame
问罪卷

(34)　The character of a law lies not in its text, but in its execution; the root of punishment lies not in how crimes are punished, but in how they are identified and framed.

(35)　Everyone can be convicted, and to add an accusation to a person must first determine the target. Crimes don't come out automatically, snitching and reporting your enemy makes the crimes come out. If there is no decree, wait patiently; if there is a decree, arrest your enemy immediately. It is common for people to assert their innocence. Interrogate them ruthlessly and punish them harshly. It is difficult for them not to plead guilty under these circumstances. If certain people who refuse to plead guilty are beaten to death, this circumstance might be explained by suicide because of fear of guilt. There is no one who does not create a network for their actions, and convicting one individual might reveal his accomplices. The defendant's confession must be immaculate, edited and mended so that it does not dispute the facts apparently. If things are done like this, not only an accusation, but a crime can be established.

(36)   Different people have different thoughts. Attack where their minds are weak to break their nerves.

(37)   The body structures of people are same, as are their feelings of dread of torture. If you torture someone with what he fears the most, he will submit definitely. You should have no mercy since those who display mercy have no indication

of their integrity; your friends should get even harsher punishments since those who aid friends can only bring danger to themselves.

(38) Using conspiracy to add crimes to others may avoid being added crimes by others. This is not easy, but you have to try.

【The original text in ancient Chinese】
【中文原文】

(34) 法之善恶，莫以文也，乃其行焉；刑之本哉，非罚罪也，乃明罪焉。

(35) 人皆可罪，罪人须定其人。罪不自招，密而举之则显。上不容罪，无谕则待，有谕则逮。人辩乃常，审之勿悯，刑之非轻，无不招也。或以拒死，畏罪释耳。人无不党，罪一人可举其众；供必无缺，善修之毋违其真。事至此也，罪可成矣。

(36) 人异而心异，择其弱者以攻之，其神必溃。

(37)　　身同而惧同，以其至畏而刑之，其
　　　　人固屈。怜不可存，怜人者无证其
　　　　忠。友宜重惩，援友者惟其害。

(38)　　罪人或免人罪，难为亦为也。

— 51 —

This page intentionally left blank.

11. Trial and Torture

刑罚卷

11. Trial and Torture
刑罚卷

(39) To send a man to his death, nothing is more successful than framing him for rebellion; to get men to confess to acts that they did not commit, only punishment may achieve the desired result. Pay close attention to the procedure: The horrifying aspect of torture is the numerous forms. If there are no limitations on the forms of punishment, everyone will confess their crimes.

(40) A sensible man fears danger, and a stupid man fears punishment. Verbal persuasions are the most effective form of trial. Smart people can understand the

existing objective condition, whilst fools continue to argue over what is reasonable and what is not. Treating others according to the requirements of the situation is the starting point for trial.

(41)   Death is acceptable, but pain is intolerable, thus choose torture techniques that they cannot endure. Scholars cannot tolerate humiliation, and common people are concerned about relating their loved ones, thus punishments towards them should consist of taking what people fear most. If they do not plead guilty, then impose a higher guilt than the original; if the evidence cannot be collected, then fake evidence as real as it is. Punishment can be ineffective, but framing is always effective: don't worry about adding crimes without legitimate reason, as long as the monarch is suspicious of your enemies, your plot is successful.

(42)   Those who are tortured will be punished inhumanely, but those who inflict pain on others will escape punishment. To be treated inhumanly is inferior and to be unpunished is superior. Inferior people are slaughtered, and superior people dominate the life and death of others. People's choice of attitudes and behaviors, probably stem from this, right?

【The original text in ancient Chinese】
【中文原文】

(39)   致人于死，莫逾构其反也；诱人以服，非刑之无得焉。刑有术，罚尚变，无所不施，人皆授首矣。

(40)   智者畏祸，愚者惧刑；言以诛人，刑之极也。明者识时，顽者辩理；势以待人，罚之肇也。

(41)   死之能受，痛之难忍，刑人取其不堪。士不耐辱，人患株亲，罚人伐其不甘。人不言罪，加其罪逾彼；

证不可得，伪其证率真。刑有不及，
陷无不至；不患罪无名，患上不疑
也。

(42) 人刑者非人也，罚人者非罚也。非
人乃贱，非罚乃贵。贱则鱼肉，贵
则生死。人之取舍，无乃得此乎？

— 57 —

This page intentionally left blank.

12. Expanding the Range of Victims

瓜蔓卷

12. Expanding the Range of Victims
瓜蔓卷[9]

(43) Things are never larger enough to be startling. There are never more people involved in the case enough for your credit to be disclosed. The monarch frames conspiracies to seek stability, while courtiers utilize it to gain credit and favor. There must be grievances, but it is impossible to avoid them.

---

[9] The direct Chinese translation of this title is: The vine of the melon. If we find the vine, we can find the melon according to a vine. This is a metaphor meaning that after a conspiracy has framed a person, it is possible to interrogate him to get him to confess other participants. The conspirator can use this to expand the circle of victims. This is what it is all about: following the vine to find the melon. I translate the title as: expanding the range of victims.

(44)   True favor may inspire others to be favored, while real disaster can relate others to disaster. Do not rely on favor that you did not earn; do not ignore someone else's crisis so that you miss the opportunity to take advantage. If there is no evidence of the crime, other crimes are used as attachments; if the wicked actions are not exposed, others' evil deeds can be utilized as evidence. Falsely accuse those who threaten you of being an ally of enemy country; portray those you despise as deceitful and evil criminals.

(45)   A friend of an official is a collaborator in the eyes of the ordinary people, who view the official as their adversary; a friend of relatives is also an enemy in the eyes of an enemy who has animosity with their relatives; thus, the enemy might change. A friend in wealth is an enemy in decline; conversely, a friend in poverty is an enemy in prosperity; hence,

friendships are also temporary. Therefore, power is not to be abandoned, and if you abandon it, you will lose your foundation; compassion is not to be given casually, and if it is, you will attract people's jealousy; you cannot be too close to people, and if you are, you will be cheated; sincere words are not to be spoken, and if you do not have any reservations, you will be in a potential danger. Wise people will not inflict injury on themselves; capable people are always searching for weaknesses of others, it is perfectly sound to lure people into taking the bait and then arrest them appropriately.

【The original text in ancient Chinese】
【中文原文】

(43)　事不至大，无以惊人。案不及众，功之匪显。上以求安，下以邀宠，其冤固有，未可免也。

(44)　荣以荣人者荣，祸以祸人者祸。荣非己莫恃，祸惟他勿纵。罪无实者，他罪可代；恶无彰者，人恶以附。心之患者，置敌一党；情之怨者，陷其奸邪。

(45)　官之友，民之敌；亲之友，仇之敌，敌者无常也。荣之友，败之敌；贱之友，贵之敌，友者有时也。是以权不可废，废则失本，情不可滥，滥则人忌；人不可密，密则疑生；心不可托，托则祸伏。智者不招己害，能者寻隙求功。饵之以逮，事无悖矣。

NOTE

1. Confucius. He was the Spring and Autumn Period Chinese philosopher who founded the Confucian school of thinking. Successive monarchs or adherents of Confucianism have venerated Confucius as a sage. China and East Asia have been tremendously influenced by Confucianism.

2. Zuo Qiuming. Per the mythology, at the end of the Spring and Autumn Period in China, he was a blind historian from the State of Lu and the creator of *The Commentary of Zuo* and *Discourses of the States*. During the Warring States period, *The Commentary of Zuo* became a classic of the Confucian school.

3. Duke Huan of Qi (? - 643 BC). The ruler of the Qi state during the Spring and Autumn era. He appointed sage professionals, cultivated productive forces, eradicated political corruption, and enhanced military capabilities. Under his

direction, the state of Qi became the first hegemon within ancient Chinese territory. In the latter years of his reign, his nomination of disloyal ministers caused such havoc in the dynasty that he was imprisoned and starved to death in his palace by the traitors. After his death, his sons descended into internecine conflict, and the empire declined.

4. Fuchai (? - 473 BC). King of the Wu State during the Spring and Autumn Period. Under his leadership, the State of Wu defeated the State of Yue, an ancient adversary; nevertheless, due to his generosity, he did not entirely destroy the State of Yue but instead imprisoned its ruler. Later, the monarch of the Yue State avenged Fu Chai by conquering the Wu State.

5. Yang Guang (569 - 618). The second emperor of China's Sui Dynasty. According to legend, he killed his father, the elderly monarch Yang Jian, and usurped power when his father was gravely sick. The old king Yang Jian is regarded as one of history's greatest monarchs.

6. Wang Mang (45 BC - 23). A prominent Chinese statesman during the Western Han Dynasty. Initially, he was acclaimed for being a respectful and morally upright minister. But upon attaining power, he eventually exposed his ambition, abolishing the Western Han Dynasty and establishing the Xin Dynasty as his own state. He is a disputed historical figure in China. During his ascent to the throne, he crushed dissenters, selected cronies, and implemented several reforms that were so ahead of their time that they were ridiculed by the people. His empire eventually succumbed to insurrection, and he was murdered by the rebels.

7. Ji Dan (? - about 1000 BC). He was active around the year 1000 BCE. He was one of the Western Zhou dynasty's founders. He supported the young emperor in constructing the empire's institutions and was the empire's true ruler. In order to prevent suspicion, he displayed extreme humility due to his immense authority.

8. Favor is a term used throughout the text to describe gathering glory and

obtaining the trust and affection of the ruler.

9. The direct Chinese translation of this title is: The vine of the melon. If we find the vine, we can find the melon according to a vine. This is a metaphor meaning that after a conspiracy has framed a person, it is possible to interrogate him to get him to confess other participants. The conspirator can use this to expand the circle of victims. This is what it is all about: following the vine to find the melon. I translate the title as: expanding the range of victims.

IIOPS
Istanbul Institute of
Political Strategy